STRANGE WITH AGE

Also by Sharon Cumberland

Peculiar Honors
The Arithmetic of Mourning
Sharon Cumberland Greatest Hits 1985-2000

STRANGE WITH AGE

Poems by
Sharon Cumberland

Black Heron Press
Post Office Box 13396
Mill Creek, Washington 98082
www.blackheronpress.com

ISBN: 978-1-936364-24-4

Several of the poems appeared in the following publications, some in slightly different versions:
"About Trees," *Nerve* 2001:10
"Accident," *The Cortland Review* 1999:5
"Another Story," *Raven Chronicles Journal* 2016:23
"He Summoned the Twelve," *Verse* 1996:13/1
"I Don't Write Nature Poems," *Midwest Quarterly* 2006:Winter
"Precentrix," Jack Straw Writers Anthology 2006:12
"Recipe," *Margie Annual* 2009:52; *Sharon Cumberland Greatest Hits 1985-2000*, Puddinghouse Publications 2002, Johnston, Ohio
"Red Hand/White Man." *Catch the Tide: New Writing from the Federation of Writers Scotland,* Glasgow: New Voices Press 2000; *Floating Bridge Review 3* Spring 2010
"Starling Road." *The Cortland Review* 1999:6

"Another Story" is inspired by Stephen Dunn's poem "Story."
"The Cradle" is a lyric written for composer John Hill, Christmas 2014.
"Consolation," "To the Saudi Student Who Left His Prayer Schedule Behind," and "My Housemate Bows A Thousand Times" won First Place in the Pacific Northwest Writer's Association poetry competition, 2012.

Poems on the life of Yeshua incorporate the fourteen end-rhyming words of the following Shakespearean sonnets:

"The Miraculous Draught of Fishes"	Sonnet 102
"The Three Temptations"	Sonnet 144
"He Summoned the Twelve"	Sonnet 91

The poet wishes to thank the Corporation of Yaddo for many years of encouragement and support, and Seattle University for two summer writing grants.

For my husband,
James Thomas Jones

Co-supremes and stars of love.

CONTENTS

IT'S HARD TO KNOW WHAT'S GOING ON

TV NEWS AT NINE

A mob is throwing rocks
and chanting something.
Their fists erupt like bubbles
boiling up in a pot of water.
Then a weeping woman
hides her face in her apron—
a husband or a father holds
a snapshot up to the camera:
a baby, possibly a boy.
Now a puppy, stuck
in a culvert, is rescued
by a fireman with a rope.
The weatherman applies
smiley faces and frowny faces
to a map. Rain cartoons
appear, then avuncular suns.
A school bus, stuck in the snow,
reveals children, their noses
pressed to the window.
Gladiators of the gridiron
tackle each other on a green
rug. A mob cheers, punching
the air together. Finally,
a woman whose hair flows
like a blonde river sits
at a desk with Our Fine City
behind her as though the studio
were perched on a cliff.
She frowns and sounds worried
then smiles, showing her teeth.
Good night! she waves. Good bye!

GONE

You curl the animal in a circle
the way she curled herself when living:
limbs folded, long tail tucked
beneath her chin. You fetch
the best pillow case
from the linen closet—never
minding that Grandma
received it for her wedding—
the old lace a tribute
to your poor animal
who loved you so.
You slide your friend,
your old friend, into her shroud,
and fold the lacework under
her body, so much heavier now.
As you place your companion
in the damp hole of your flower
border you seem to hear a whistle
from a far place, as if your ears
can hear, like hers did, a high call
from the land where she's gone.

MY MOTHER'S BRACELET

In the village of Labaro, on the patio of a pink villa
my mother sits alone. The static Tiber
and Sabine Hills lie flat in the distance. My father
is at work. I'm playing hooky, wandering
the backstreets of Rome,
slow to come home.

In the stillness of a long afternoon she contemplates
the charms on her bracelet: Cairo, Jerusalem, Beirut.
She sailed on the Constitution, rode a camel in Gaza,
climbed the Sagrada Familia. On her wrist a Coliseum,
a Parthenon, the falling pillars of Byblos.
She lifts a third Manhattan to her lips
and the little cowbell from Switzerland tinkles.
A mist of spirits drowse her: Cathedral of Cologne,
a gondola, the Matterhorn. She reclines like Cleopatra
on her barge, the Caesar of a golden world.
She is crossing the Himalyas on an elephant;
she is discovering the Dead Sea.

TRICK OR TRUTH

She wore a naked suit in Times
Square complete with fake-fur
pubic hair and two pink buttons
sewn to the flesh-colored leotard
restraining her breasts. Strangers
turned away, shocked, thrilled!
Traffic jammed and ogled—
an impressive mess even
for Times Square on a high
October noon.
       "Indecent exposure!" the cop
said, seizing her pink-clad
bicep, "You're under arrest."
"But officer," she cooed, "I'm totally
covered, from top to Jimmy Choos!"
Nevertheless—fenders bent, tourists
went back to Cleveland and Butte,
Sodom & Gomorrah confirmed.
       So what, dear reader, did the judge decree
concerning abstract nudity? "Fire!" in a crowded theater?
Or Ms. Go-diva, *faux* birthday suit intact,
released to trouble traffic another day?

PIRANESI: VEDUTA DELLA PIAZZA DEL POPOLO

It wasn't mud in my day, when I waited at the base
of the Flaminio obelisk for my father to pick me up
after school in his Austin Princess, whirling
around the piazza with the Fiat cinquecentos
like colorful bathing suits in a tumble dryer.
Italian boys whistle at my thighs peeking
between pleated skirt and knee socks. I try
to ignore them, but my smile—Venus surprised!—
makes them call to my father as he pulls over
in his chic little car: *Buona fortuna, vecchio!*

WHEN A FRESH, YOUNG GIRL

I was crazy, coy.
I would lure a boy into Lambda Woods
and make him desperate,
drawing him with my hands into that lost moment:
loss of awareness,
loss of control,
—then slap him—
—hard—
and leave him: drawers down,
entangled in moss and leaves,
calling to me as the ocean of woods
widened in my wake,
a faint, baffled call
like a faltering bird,
or the dove
surrounded by losses,
solitary
in the emptying world.

RED HAND/WHITE MAN

In New York, they don't mince words.
The signs on the corners say WALK
or they say DON'T WALK. The people
then do as they please.
In Seattle, the situation is less direct.
There are symbols on the corners—
these could mean anything.
For instance, one symbol is a Red Hand,
palm out, like an Indian Chief.
It seems to say "How"
or even "Peace, Kimo Sabe!"
Could it be that this is the hand
of Chief Seattle, greeting you gravely,
cordially, at every corner?
      But suddenly, the hand grows agitated,
as though the Chief is no longer peaceful
and might lunge for your neck with a yelp!
His hand, which was merely red before,
now appears to be bloody. It flashes
faster and faster, as if pushing you backwards.
This may mean that you, with your briefcase,
your grocery bag, or your child by the hand
pose some inscrutable threat,
so that now his hand seems abject
and pleading: STOP! STOP!
      But then another symbol appears:
a White Man, striding. This man faces West.
This man swings his arms—he is a whole man,
not just a piece of a man like the Indian Chief.
This man has legs. He has a head.
How can the disembodied Red Hand
stand up to this? The White Man says WALK

*

to the corner, WALK to the Bay.
WALK to the ends of the earth!
   The Red Hand and the White Man
contend on every corner. Who, in Seattle,
can cross the street in peace?

WATCHING OTHERS PRAY

is like watching sleepers or day dreamers.
They slide and slump in chairs, eyes closed,
or sit erect wearing life masks
of themselves. Some ponder
with open eyes cast down, or frown
as though they doubt that God
is, or is good. But the little boy
in the red-rimmed glasses
stares all around, looks straight
at everyone.

Some pray the Lord's Prayer with palms
unfolded, raised to the acoustic tile,
or with hands clasped over crotch
as if to disguise the rogue body.
Some hold hands with strangers,
make steeples with their fingers,
or hide fists in the pits of their arms.
But the little girl in rubber sandals
swings her feet, laces her fingers
between her mother's rings.

Some take communion with their hands
in cups like thirsty hikers, some
stick tongues out at the priest
who feeds them slivers. Others
look her in the eye and smile,
or refuse to look, shy canines.
But the boy with the hurricane hair
chomps his bread like a hamburger bun,
knowing it's common—there's always more
where that came from.

LEFT BEHIND

Wet streets at 3 AM.
I follow him to the hospital
in a separate car. He insisted
on driving himself to the side
of his third wife who may not
last the night. He signals right
and turns left. I see his elbow lift
to clear the windshield or wipe
his eyes. At eighty-seven
he had a right to think the world
would outlive him—no more deathbed
watches or sudden loss of child, wife,
or hope. How he cries at her bedside now,
the bed that fills and empties.

MY HOUSEMATE BOWS A THOUSAND TIMES

It's what they do at her Korean temple
when something is amiss with the spirit:
kneel, bend head to rug,
lift hands palms up
then stand again,
like a river flowing backward,
before falling forward once more
on your knees
in a smooth wave.
She will do this a thousand times
to expiate the anger in her breast
at her professor, who makes her work
long hours in the laboratory,
who shouts at her,
takes credit for her research—the man
she tries not to hate.
If she bows a thousand times
he will shrink in the waves of worship
that wash her soul.
It takes twelve hours
to bow away the man
who tries to bend her
to his will.

IT'S HARD TO KNOW WHAT'S GOING ON

I said, as I placed my cat in its grave.
For two weeks I wiped her bloody mouth,
squirted water down her throat
with an ear syringe until I finally saw
it was no use. The veterinarian came,
was extremely kind, threaded the needle
through the vein, knowing who was doing
the suffering. It was easy enough to see life end,
her furry head drooping, her eyes half-shut,
her paw now so willing to be held, like little girls
holding hands, or lovers strolling along,
their private delight on public display.
But what, she asked the sandy earth piled
in the back yard by the others under their stones,
is going on here? What of mysterious
promises? of heaven for cats and dogs?
Reincarnation? Resurrection?
The earth inhales and takes her.
That much is clear.

THE THREE TEMPTATIONS

He was not only hungry, but lost. The desert
is the same in all directions. Despair set in.
He could neither walk nor sit still. Then
a man appeared from the air—so graceful,
so fair—that Yeshua believed it was an angel.
You look ill, it said. *Share my meal.*

With that, a banquet—not just bread—
but leg of lamb, mint sauce, nectarines,
honey and figs was spread on the desert floor.
Yeshua felt a rush of relief: *The evil is behind me!*
He thanked God and reached toward the manna.

But the man with sapphire eyes handed him
a stone. *Look!* it said, *how easy!* caressing
the stone into roasted goat: charred, mouthwatering,
fragrant. Yeshua felt the scratch of danger
down his spine, turned from the devil
to face the wilderness again.

Beside him the man with the delicate hands
said *Come, now, your pride will kill you!*
Its outspread arms made the desert
the world—glittering, needy. *They hunger for you.*
The fiend spoke in a voice like cymbals.
Yeshua sat down in the hot sand, rubbing
his eyes. *It's true, they need me*
he told his Father. *What should I do?*

The man with feet like ivory said: *Look, friend!*
The ground fell away. They were on the Temple roof.
The desert below was Jerusalem.

*

Go to them, it said. *Fly down to your people.*
(The press of his sinuous fingers
on Yeshua's back). *The Son of God can do anything!*
Yeshua could see it all, a pageant spread over
the sand, forward and back. He faced the wondrous
man and said: *You're right, I can.*
He embraced the demon who, he realized, was as needy
as any. *Go back to Hell*, said Yeshua, *I'll be there shortly.*

Rage, then doubt, then the squint of anticipation
marred the devil's golden brow
before he led the Rabbi out.

CLAIRE DE LUNE

MY PHANTOM CHIDREN

call me *Mami!* or *Papá!*
since all things are possible
in dreams. I embrace them
together—Estella, Angel—
or kiss them one-by-one.
For some reason I am
Spanish, and not sad
my children are insubstantial,
that they cannot eat strawberries
or nap in the back of the car.
It doesn't matter. We live
in Sevilla, strolling narrow lanes,
wearing polka-dot kerchiefs,
where jasmine overpowers the air
drooping over balconies.
I wish my spaniel could lick
the sweet faces of my children
with her pink tongue—
the little spaniel, Esperanza,
I will someday adopt.

LOOKING BACKWARD

Pink roses cascade over a white picket fence
like decorations on a wedding cake:
My God—it's the worst kind of cliché.
Yet I want to rub those roses
all over my face, to dive naked
into those pink roses until love scratches
cover my body.
                      Red roses on a brick wall
would not conjure this desire. No—
I want to make love only to those pink roses
cascading over that white picket fence.
They disappear into my rear view mirror.

WEIGHTS

There was a dead cat
in my backyard this morning.
I don't often see a dead thing.
I put it in a trash bag
thinking: it is surprisingly
heavy. Then my mind leapt
to you—your lean body, your
goatee, your cat's tongue and its
prowling. You weigh so little
on me; yet this feline—oddly
heavy when it goes. Well, well.
It will bear down soon enough.
But for now, my creature, you—
you, and light-footed life.

PINK TULIPS

Six pink tulips, each petal
ribboned white,
fan out from my painted vase.
Laura put them there
from love,
but their future is not
bright. Soon
they will flag and bend
and lose their heads.
But today they are
alabaster and pink onyx,
standing erect like
six rosy princesses in green gowns,
or like
six glasses of grenadine in milk,
or like
a rumpled green bed with six pink pillows
strewn invitingly
with six green arms
and six pink hands that are open
open open open open open

SALZACH RIVER ROUND

We sit under lindens sipping coffee. The old river
rushes to town between mountains, playing chords
over rocks—the same river, green as a dirndl,
that Mozart heard as a boy, running to its banks
to sail his skiff, to fish for rainbow trout.

Though old it never tires, rushing to town
past this Gasthaus built when Salzburg
was surrounded by woods. Green as a dirndl
in a sky-colored apron, The Salzach tumbles past—
plays the water-opera Mozart heard as a boy.

We watch it rush to the Hohensalzburg castle,
its battlements loom over Mozart's town,
crenellations like muffled drums on a green field.
We sip coffee as the river sings—Pamina,
Susana, Dorabella—Mozart heard them as a boy,

saw the march of Mustafa, Figaro, the relentless Don
himself looming over the town, the river—green
as a dirndl—lifting its apron of clouds. Sipping coffee
we hear the voice of the Salzach, the boom of the castle,
while rainbow trout teem in the river he knew as a boy.

SEA OF LILACS

I saw a sea of lilacs
with a school of black bees
swimming from bloom to bloom
black with yellow noses
like clownfish
humming through purple waves
a forest of thin stalks
waved beneath them
in breezy currents.
What kind of creature
would I have to be
to glide into those green stems
with a flick?
Something clothed
in its own form
as are lilacs,
like a bee.

ABOUT TREES

They are bigger than we are, and slower. They grow
every day at a pace we can't notice. Trees do not act: they are
acted upon. Do you think the beech or the aspen
is tossing its leaves in the wind? No—the earth creates currents
in air that simulate dance. Trees
neither dance nor make music with their leaves. They are instruments,
like clarinets or kettle drums: they wait for hurricanes and woodpeckers
to play them. Yet, like the Stradivarius, a tree cannot hear itself.
Trees are deaf. Their rustling, tapping, the high notes of rain
dripping bough upon bough is lost upon them.
A tree cannot hear squirrels scamper their nails along its side,
or the crow clearing its throat. Furthermore, trees are blind.
Bluebirds, parakeets, rufous-breasted cockatoos may as well be sleet gray
for all a tree knows. Its own leaves—fuchsia, turquoise—are blank
transparencies to a tree. The gum cannot taste its chicle, nor the maple
its syrup; a pine does not smell its perfume, sharp as needles
rising around it in the rain.
Instead, they feel. Trees are entirely tactile. They know birds by weight
and claw—the heavy ones, the tickling ones, the ones who burrow
with something pointed. Squirrels are a pattern of prickling roads; monkeys
are scattering rhythms; the sleeping leopard heft, only heft.
Trees get cold get warm their fluids rise and fall. Trees die so slowly
they can't notice, can't hear or taste it coming, can't smell something sour
or see the brown patch creeping down the limb. They don't know they
are gnarled,
that their roots are poking through the sidewalk, that creatures cluster in
their shade
or feast on their fruit. Time is nothing to a tree, they are so much bigger
than we are, so much slower.

I DON'T WRITE NATURE POEMS

Not because I don't admire nature—
I do. At seventeen,
in Switzerland,
I'd go alone from camp and climb
the highest Alpine trail I knew,
to stare at sights extravagantly
vast. They pushed me back
from cliffs of future burdens
with their larger emptiness.
But that was twenty years ago.
Now my Brooklyn window
gives a view of trees in concrete
intervals. My patch of sun comes round
like a grocery boy. My garden
is a spider plant. For years
it couldn't grow and wouldn't die—
a balance with no deficit, and no
spider shoot to justify it.
Unlike the sun, I had enough
of nourishing—I hacked the leaves away
and dropped it on my fire escape
and forgot it. Two weeks after that
it was bristling green; a fortnight later
a spider tendril jumped away—
Sudden!—like an Alpine geyser
sprung from the rocks. Or rather,
a wild strawberry, sweet as bee stings,
nestling in a crevice
on Jungfrau's peak.

TROPES OF ODYSSEUS

He sleeps on my left shoulder.
He isn't heavy—I could bear his weight
all night. He shifts his head
onto my breasts and snores a bit,
his breath filling my cleavage, his legs
curled around my legs.
His hands twitch, as if describing
our heat in his dream.
       Sleeper, do you know
what flows from your body
into my body? The laws
of gravity, electromagnetic
exchanges of energy,
tropes of Odysseus
(his loss, his Nausicaän plea),
and the Trojans—searching,
searching for Rome—
their most lasting discovery.

I HAVE A PLEASANT FACE

        or so people say when they greet me
in the narthex, certain they have met me
before—or strolling the lobby at intermission,
or at the coffee counter in the bookstore—
one of those faces you see everywhere
and notice when you need someone
to sit with on the bus, or on a park bench,
before moving on.
        I was at Smart Alec's on Telegraph,
eating lentil soup when a woman approached ,
sat down, said she saw me through the window,
as though my profile were a door inscribed
"Welcome." She had too many bags, she hobbled
a bit, her roots were showing, she graduated
from Berkeley forty years ago, first time back,
was shocked at the "toilet" Telegraph had become.
        I wondered. as she rambled on, if Jesus
ever sighed then set his book aside for someone
seeking a spot in the shade by a friendly face.
Did he force his mind to focus on the rambling
story before him, the tale of disappointment
and fatigue? The account of the bus fare,
the lost wallet, the dead husband, the children
in Chicago, too far away to pay attention?
How did he sacrifice the time, who had so little?
        I'm over sixty now, my purse of time
is lighter. How to be content, spending it
on strangers who by my pleasant face
feel free to take a coin? How to give alms
without sighing as I push aside *War and Peace*
or *The Remains of the Day*?

CANVAS SKIN

At the art museum: "Contemporary Tattoos."
A photo gallery of life-sized nudes clothed
in parti-colored skin. Nowhere do I see the bare
grandeur of marble Zeus, of snowy-breasted
Venus, or David's stainless, straining limbs.

No—these folks are trapped in jumbled vines,
bellies be-dragoned, bottoms feathered with crows.
They seem marred to me—me, whose aging skin
for all its wrinkles and childhood scars remains intact,
un-mermaided, un-*Mother*ed—entirely my own.

On these walls these bodies are inert as framed linen,
each stitch a red dot, then a black stain. Images
accumulate, but who benefits from your pain?
Does the canvas—obedient to the needle—collaborate
with an amateur or with a Michelangelo?

You there, inkbound in muddy glory: who
would you be, free of the etchings worked on you?
Your skin—once free as a baby's—is now patterned
like pajamas. Would Zeus ever wear such gear, or Venus?
You herald the new gods of your needled universe.

POEM ENDING WITH A PHRASE FROM "L'ALLEGRO"

When you get a magazine,
first shake out all the blow-ins
and rip out all the bind-ins,
even the ones bound in so hard
they leave a dragon's back
along the spine.
That makes it yours.
Then flip through the pages backwards
which eliminates logic and order.
There were never such things.
Look in the faces of those purified girls
whose pores have been eliminated
along with the ordinary.
Examine their spiked sandals
and conical breasts,
the red-laced patent-leather capri pants,
the mouth like a beckoning vagina.
This is Arcadia: the shepherdess,
the pipes, the fat green lea,
even the silly sheep are there,
gazing out with their tranquil
vacancy. Lie down
in your magazine; roll in the soft
perfection of it. Feast
on the abundance covering
every page before returning,
refreshed,
to the busy hum of men.

CLAIR DE LUNE

Take back the baby mug with the misspelled
name: "Clara" not "Clare." The moon sheds light
on my upturned face, though my taxes are overdue.

The moon turns to sky, slides over an invisible horizon;
violets bloom one-by-one in the slice of sun
shining through a side window. Overdue taxes loom.

I hang a paisley scarf over the curtain rod
as the sun slides through my side window.
Clara, not Clare. Newspapers pile up by the door,

bills heap my desk, the light slides through a side
window past the paisley scarf on my curtain rod.
Sort blue envelopes and yellow envelopes, bills

heaped with bad news, misspelled baby mug, taxes
overdue. Moon, sliding over the invisible horizon,
violets bloom. Clara, not Clare—the moon on my upturned face.

SITTING ON THE POET'S CHAIR AT THE GLOBE IN DUMFRIES

It's a wee dark room, once smoky, once crowded
with jocular ploughmen at their ale and claret.
The chair by the hearth is triangular, small
by our standards—the seat of the man
who said for his folk what they could not say,
and said it better. Here Robert Burns held sway,
those two hundred years ago, and here am I,
on the poet's chair today, grinning faces
expecting me to recite all the verses of "Auld Lang Syne"
or "Scots Wha Hae". *O my luv is like
a red, red, rose,* I try—but it's not enough.
They wait for more; they whisper hints and phrases
to the pur poet from America. Not much
is expected from me but goodwill. We laugh, climb up
to the bedroom where the Bard of Ayershire
ploughed a different field. We stare at the box bed,
narrow by our standards—humble drunken fun and trouble.
What survives becomes sacred with time.

THE MIRACULOUS DRAUGHT OF FISHES

Simon can't refuse without seeming rude.
So what if we've already trolled all night, and for nothing?
When the crowds appear in the morning, trailing the Rabbi
like shoals of sprats—Simon put the Rabbi into the boat
to preach until the people floated away.
    Then Simon hopes to get some rest, and mend his nets,
but no—the Rabbi springs up and insists that they fish again.
God of Jonah! Simon thinks. *What carpenters know*
about fishing could feed a sardine!
But he bites his tongue and they lay into the oars
while the Rabbi leans over the side, sings to his reflection.
He wouldn't be so jolly if he had to fish
for a living, thinks Simon. He is crabby:
it's been days since they caught anything.
    But now the water turns solid—Simon can't move
his oars through the density of fins: tunny and cod,
salmon and plate-like flounder. They crowd the boat
like nightfall. Simon flings the nets over the side. He calls
to his partners, but the boat is already sinking at the bow.
They cut the nets—too late! The fish are up to their thighs,
their waists! It is punishment for greed—too much of a good thing.
Simon can't kneel to repent for the pilchard and squid
twining his legs. *Master!* he cries. *Leave me! I'm a sinner!*
    But the Rabbi is lost in delight, sliding his bare arms
through the mound of brine and sole, salt on his tongue,
scales in his hair. He carols to the anchovies
and bream in his arms. His song sounds to Simon
like *eels or pickerel* or *fishy people* or maybe, yes,
he hears him now—*we'll fish for my bounty of people.*

MY FATHER HAS GROWN STRANGE WITH AGE

SUNDAY MORNING BEFORE CHURCH

My godlike father with all his hair
is planted with his subjects on his lawn:
my mother in her slender suit, like Hera
in spitcurls; my godmother in final bloom,
dimpling for my uncle hunched over
the camera; we three kids arranged in front
like caryatids, supporting all their pride:
my sister with her golden hair and skirt
too long, my brother beaming—
his father's heir, the favored, only son.
And I—on tiptoes, straining to exceed
my brother's height, the only solemn face.
My intention drills the camera: taller,
smarter, taller, stronger—lovelier
than Hera, even. More solid than the god.

HOLY POVERTY

It was the Feast of St. Helena,
our patroness—a Friday. I was cellarer's
assistant with a long list for the Pathmark
grocery, the liquor store, the bakery.
Twenty for dinner: Rock Cornish game hens,
asparagus tips, poppy seed rolls, two gallons
of rosé. Sister Paula's specialty was tiramisu,
so I had to buy *Sealtest* ice cream—nothing
else would do unless I cared to face
her wrath. I had to be back by tea at four
or vespers at the latest. I wore my habit
to save changing—my long skirts flapping
behind a wire basket stacked with hens
and olives and artichoke hearts, my veil
pursuing me as I rushed through the aisles.
Last stop—the ice cream case—
there I piled half gallons of Sealtest
into my cart with both hands—two, four, six—
beside a young mother picking through pints
of cheap sorbet. She turned each one over
to peer at the price, her kids on tip-toes,
chins tipped up like little wrens.
"No, Mommy! Please!" they cried
when she left empty-handed,
herding them away.

Hands full, I froze to watch them go
as the motes fell. Did Helena stand
this way in Jerusalem, seeing those footfalls
on the suffering road? She raised a basilica
wherever the veil trembled—but who was I,

46

a novice in the grocery aisle? Vespers called,
and Sister Paula's tapping foot—duty, routine,
obedience. It took another year to shed my habit,
to follow that mother down the road.

MY FATHER HAS GROWN STRANGE WITH AGE:
A CROWN OF SONNETS

(1)

My father has grown strange with age. He sees
from his great distance things beyond himself,
as if his world were overlaid: the breeze
I feel, for him a threatening draft; the shelf
of sleep, for him a precipice—the cliff
he must step off of. Death is a long gown
he wears on bended shoulders, thick and stiff.
This livelihood of dying weighs him down,
distracts him into odd remarks, like "God
forgives us for our thoughtless livings" or
"My angel's name is Sam." I smile and nod—
I'm glad it's making sense to him. He's more
the father to his pregnant self than me,
so tasked with giving birth to death is he.

(2)

So tasked with giving birth to death is he,
my father lets the live world disappear
before his fading eyes. Why should he see
what matters little now? He wants to hear
the choir of angels he was taught to love
in childhood, meet St. Peter with his keys,
then enter New Jerusalem—the glove
of resurrection fitted over his disease
to re-enflesh his soul—trusting that God
forgives the tearful sinner. I wonder,
when his blue eyes flicker out, and the nod
of death brings chin to chest, if there—under
the bed or in a corner of the room—
transparent midwives birth him from this womb?

(3)

Transparent midwives birth him from this womb
of three dimensions—high and wide and deep—
to realms past proof, as once the black room
of his mother was a kingdom of sleep
and surety, before the sudden *smack*—
when light imposed, appalled, his new domain.
He shrieked! He shrank from the attack
of giant forms, horrors of color. In
air, it felt like drowning—a tadpole scooped
from oozy shallows. Yet catastrophe
is masked as sudden endings—fear enlooped
with swags of mystery. Reality
is stranger: new life in the death of things,
when frogs shed tails and moths unfurl their wings.

(4)

"'When frogs shed tails, the moths unfurl their wings'—
that's what your Grandpa Cumbie used to say,"
Dad said to me, *apropos* of nothing.
"I don't want to celebrate my birthday.
Good heavens, you kids make such a fuss. Why,
when I was a boy, in the Depression,
we made our own root beer, you couldn't buy
presents. We made everything. Mom's lemon
cake was a treat when we could get the fruit.
I juiced them with Grandma's wooden reamer."
He smiled, then noticed me. "You kids were cute.
Two brainy ones—good luck!—and one dreamer.
That's you." He sees me through the fog of time,
a glimpse—and then returns to the sublime.

49

(5)

A glimpse—and then he turns to the sublime,
where I don't fit, a world he bids at will—
where his mother is sane and in her prime,
his wife is slim and sober, the downhill
slide forgiven. "Dearest Ree," he wrote her
in V-mail, "I'll earn my admiral's stripes—
we'll do great things before we ship anchor!"
Oh, the ideal past—heaven in tintypes
of a better world. Or maybe not. What
do I know, after all? At ninety years
he's fully grown, aware—his losses cut.
He bears no grudges now. If he has tears
they are for us, his unchurched children—dumb
to the glories of what we should become.

(6)

On the glories of what we should become
I turn my back—fat chance a rosary
or sweet-faced Madonna with her winsome
babe will speak to me, or angels' airy
wings flap within my hearing. I was raised
Episcopalian by this very man himself
whose mid-life turn to Rome left us amazed—
the sudden piety—so strange—a shelf
of platitudes that required his dusting.
"I sit at the feet of God" he tells me.
"Sam's a big help. My heart is un-rusting."
His heart was always good, I think, but he
forgets how well he did in raising me.
I sometimes wish that Sam would let him be.

(7)

I sometimes wish that Sam would let him be.
I liked suburban Christianity—
faith like a dinner roll, sips of sherry.
Angels breaking rank is like your house key
opening the door onto an abyss—
a betrayal of the rules of conduct
between here and wherever heaven is.
Far be it from the daughter to instruct
the ancient dad, however—I have got
at least enough belief to trust that God
gives old folks what they need to live their lot
through. And I know that when his dear old pod
of a body is one with the graveyard tree
my father, who's grown strange with age, will see.

MY BROTHER MEETS EISENHOWER, 1956

Eleven, brown as a coconut, Johnny delivered
the *Key West Sun* with our father's
Washington Post newsboy bag slung
over one shoulder. Like Don Larsen pitching
a perfect game he hurled paper rolls
at doorways along Flagler Ave
in the hot breeze, to the applause
of rattling palm leaves. A long black car
slid beside him, a uniformed driver
called him to the curb: "Son, someone
wants to speak with you."
A back window rolled down.
The president's avuncular face—the sun
in *e pluribus unum*—beamed out at him.
"Where did you get that bag, my boy?
It's a long way from home!"

Not until halfway through dinner—sloppy joes,
peas-and-carrots, jello salad—did he tell
our parents about the friendly President,
the black limo, show the autographed receipt
stuffed in a pocket of his dungarees.
What did a boy know of the catastrophes
that drove our parents' wartime marriage?
Dad a young man at sea, Mom a bride haunted
by empty chairs around their neighbors'
tables? Now here, in sunny Florida—Eisenhower!
Their hero of disaster and progress,
of D-Day, of ears strained
toward crackling radios? *Oh, Johnny!*
our mother cried—(he should have
hurtled through the house shouting his news)
—*Why didn't you tell us?*

We stared at our parents, their welling
tears and grins like the bright rains
of Key West when you don't know
whether to bask or take cover. We
shrugged. It was another one of those
mysteries it would take decades
to uncover.

MOM ADRIFT

Daddy left her in the lobby
"just for a while," he said,
for respite, to do laundry
(she requires so much care).
I can see her sitting there,
her coif somewhat lopsided
from the long nap she inhabits,
her ankles crossed, hands dainty
in her lap, gazing with her misty
stare that says she knows what she's doing there
(though her brain struggles to recall—
peers from behind her glasses for a clue)
when a tour bus rolls up.

Mom forgot she was senile, incontinent,
forgot she couldn't walk,
so she got on the bus for the beach,
the casino, the Confederate grave yard,
some such place. Daddy told me later
how the driver came and got him, how he
had to persuade her she wasn't
going anywhere, and led her
down the aisle like he once did
fifty years ago.
"Did you do that, Mom?" I ask.
"Oh, yes," she says.
Though he tells her and tells her
that their traveling days are over,
she thinks she still belongs
to that other world. She persists
in refreshing her lipstick
before she goes to bed.

WOW WOW WOW

is what my father says when he sees me
from his hospital bed: Wow!
Wow! Wow! and he juts
his withered old thumb
up in the air. He has forgotten
his proper nouns: *When those people*
went from where they were
to where they were going
he says, meaning when his parents,
Opal and Cumbie, left H Street
and moved to Newton Street
why, I was—I was there
and the school was over there
and the place where you got
candy was over there. Wow!
He goes from DC to Orlando
to the Naval Academy to Rome
in no particular order. *It's like*
a crazy quilt, he tells me, *you never*
know what patch you land on
from one minute to the next.
Now he's toddling down Newton Street,
now spooning soup into my senile mother
at Huntcliffe Summit, now on the gun deck
of the USS Bristol, now driving
mom and me to Ostia Antica
in the old Austin Princess
a foreign service officer sold him
for 200,000 lira. *You're gonna like it, Sharon,*
he says, pointing skyward. *You never know*
where you go next.

OLD MAN PATIENCE
After van Gogh

Hands like turtles in their rough shells
rest on a stick absent its tree these many
years. In his face, cheeks with caves
lead to silent lips. What is there to say?
Why smile at grief? He only stares
as if to say *Hello old killer.*
He's neither frightened nor surprised.
Under his straw-brimmed chapeau
he's seen the messengers—the orange
that stalks, the blue that embraces.
His red neckerchief and sleeves say
Life is noose and handcuffs. Only wait.

NIGHTMARE

MISSING IN ACTION

Often I am left with first
letters, as if clutching
the empty sweater
of a word that has fallen
over a cliff. My brain
fills in: pointing at spuds;
I say *Pass the…piano*
or, on the bus: *My car
is in the…garbage.*
　　　　　I never forget
a face. *This is my niece,*
I introduce (who I held
at the font thirty years ago,
whose wedding I danced at,
whose baby I dandle). *Her name
begins with L.*
　　　　　I and her mother, another L,
stroll in Bloomington. We lift
our eyes to the chapel,
its steeple a red hat
on a tall neck of Indiana limestone.
My sister says *Look at that…*
("steeple" is over a cliff)
…pointy church thing.
I'm sure there are more lines to this
…pancake…but
I can't think
of them just now.

MY RIGHT EYE

Looks like the left eye, looks like
a happy marriage, but
inside the jelly lies
an island of trouble:
a flotilla of aliens like witches flying
on bicycles, or dump trucks, basilisks,
a whole garage full of muddy tools
inside my eye. I try to gaze around them,
the blurs, the floaters,
so close I can't see if they're
flattened futons or bottles of beer.
I'm looking out a dirty window—
I dodge my head this way and that.
How they mar my vision, these floaters,
like corpses in a river.
They force me to remember
my body is dying, jelly first.
I don't mind, really, except
that my opportunity
to see Mt. Rainier clearly,
with the fresh eyes, the sharp eyes
of a child, was lost before I ever got here.
Good-bye, things of this earth,
found in the frail right eye.

HOME OF THE BURROWING OWL
Chromogenic print by Ann Hughes, 2001

In this photo we see houses built in what appears
to be a desert—bare hills rise in the background
against a relentless sky. The houses look large
and costly, the kind that seem so American
to people watching sit-coms and mysteries
in Spain or Greece or Mumbai: big windows,
high archways leading to basketball hoops,
courtyards of cars, refrigerators full of milk,
Coca Cola, steak. Only later, as you speculate
on who lives in these generous houses,
do you notice a mound of marl in the foreground,
a little heap of sand and gravel forming a cave
with a perfect archway. The sun casts
a shadow deep inside where a small creature
lives—we might imagine a Palladian prairie dog
or a lizard of some description. How surprised
we are to read on the caption that it is the home
of the burrowing owl. We think of owls—
their massive wingspans—as dominating
the red barn, the Douglas fir, the redwood,
or as terrorizing small creatures who burrow.
Yet here we find a humble owl, whose gravel house
is worthless to the wealthy householders
who live behind it except as occupying
land that might sell, when developed,
for more houses than we can imagine
in Manilla, Nairobi, Sana'a, or Mumbai.

WHEN I WAS POOR

I paced the sidewalks
looking for quarters.
I appeared at friends' houses
around dinner time,
my coat lined with newspapers.
I sucked on pebbles
and sold apples on the corner,
I washed windshields
at stop lights, slept under
the overpass, a bottle of Thunderbird
clutched to my chest.
I played the harmonica
on the subway and passed the hat
for change. I sat in the shelters
until dawn and checked into hospitals —
the poor man's hotel.
I ate soup at St. Mary's
and spaghetti at the Salvation
Army. My soul was preached unto
for sandwiches at the Union Gospel Mission.
My feet swelled up and I got a bad cough.
I sat on a gurney in a flimsy gown
while some young doctor in emergency
practiced on me. They might have put me
in a pauper's grave when I died,
but how would I know? Since
I wasn't hungry anymore,
I finally got some rest.

RECIPE

TAKE one boy, seven, garbage-
bag brown; PUT styrofoam grease-
fries in hand, feet in detritus
on Union Street. ADD frenzied
Ma: fat shorts, jobless, no help
from nobody and damn gimme-boy
like a curse, no fault no fault
of hers. HEAT to 96 degrees
on gummy pavement, burnt
feet and cheap poly-shirt
sweat-melting, no-bra chafing
welts. DROP accidental sweat-slippery
kid-finger fries on sidewalk,
then WALK white man on top, and breezy-
clean silk lady to MASH brown-
boy fries. Ma will IGNITE like
friction-fire; moneyless shrill-scream
will razor-flay guilt-boy.
Walkers will shock, stare; boy
will vomit inward, paralyze
and fear pool out, freezing
passers-by. Now, BREAK stun-moment
and REMOVE white silk to café,
passers-by to job-stores. LEAVE
boy in crazy Ma-oven, FEED slag-
fuel (fury and trashburgers) ten years,
then SERVE. Burnt-boy fodder good
for cop-judge iron-cage filler.

SHE INVITES ME FOR A BIKE RIDE

Her sleek helmet looks athletic, professional.
Mine feels like a styrofoam hat for the disabled.
The country road curves under the spinning blue sky.
She speeds up the hill, her white shirt disappearing
over the crest, around bends, behind evergreen boughs.
I try to follow, but pain spears my ribs and calves,
needles my lungs. Soon I am alone in the spreading landscape,
panting under a flock of clouds, along empty fields.
I accept the sympathy of scattered cows
and the occasional gazing horse. I wonder
if my heart is failing, see myself flopped in a ditch,
head in lamb's wort and jewelweed, the blue bike
idle between my legs. Sometimes I get off and push uphill,
find her waiting for me at the cross roads like a good god,
looking kindly down.

And it occurs to me,
through the tears of sweat in my eyes,
that this is like poetry:
she enticingly ahead, I panting behind,
she disappearing entirely, I wondering if I only imagined
she was there, she appearing suddenly to say
"This way, this way," then — *zoom* —
gone again.

PICASSO KNEW MY PARENTS

See Picasso's etching of a woman with a drink?
She sinks into the table like so many
triangles–elbows, knuckles, a bony jaw.
The man behind her sees his destiny
clutched in a jigger: a German girl escaping
through a glass. She drags the man with her
by the love fetter. Where does she go?
The table they lean on (spills and bottles)
seems like a cliff. With great effort
he could have pulled back and said *Enough!*
But no...so over they went,
through her little glass window together.
I thought I saw light, she cried, *like a door ajar
in the distance.* You can see in her eyes,
wide like headlights, that it was not
a window after all. Oh, her hand is a talon!
And the man is beyond weeping,
a disaster through the heart.
I know more—but how can I speak calmly
against a poor girl betrayed so thoroughly?

THE UNCHURCHING OF BROOKLYN

Whose spires once stood like generals
among these ranks of houses:
row upon row in brownstone uniforms,
flowerboxes like medals at the window-breast;
the world one congregation:
the certain, the worshipping
Borough of Churches.

Whose current congregation
own these condominiums
embellished by gothic artifacts:
arrange Haitian pillows and coffee tables
beneath figures of martyrs
surviving in stained glass.
Unaware of original names:
Saint Paul's, Saint James,
Norwegian Seaman's Church,
The Spanish Church of the Nazarene.
Unknowingly suspended
in the corner of an apse, in sacristies,
in oratories, or bits of soaring nave;
unaware of who was married, baptized,
saved or buried where they microwave
a Lean Cuisine or shave their legs.
I wonder if heaven has headquarters,
where each spent case of a church
is removed from a map of the field?
Do mighty trumpets sound retreat
defeated by the fifth column of real estate?
Or are the Principalities
and Powers still deployed:

bright liv'ried angels
gazing in converted windows
watching the electric toothbrush whirr,
as vigilant, as attentive as ever?

ACCIDENT

(1)

    Because a man bought beer at 9 AM;
because he had a few on site—fifteen
flights of girders up—before his
morning coffee break (his lips were numb,
his fingers buzzed);
    Because he felt entitled to his
morning brew, as much as to
his union contract (only beer
could soothe the acid
in his stomach as he rode a rusty
lift each day to join the platform crew).
    Because of that an accident—
a board—got loose,
got kicked, slipped off
twirled away like a paddle wheel
through a current, now toward
the park, now toward Fifty-eighth Street,
spinning on its axis
like a pinwheel on a breeze.
    The man watched it slowly,
watched it slowly fall,
because what falls is fate
whether tool or fabric
in the building trade. The board
turned upright at the end, as if
a hunter had plunged a spear
into a pond of fish
    It hit someone near a bank on Broadway.
Overhead, the man felt for his hardhat, then
his face as the fellow's head on the sidewalk
sheared away from it torso. He thought
the crowd that formed so fast

looked like minnows feeding,
as if he'd dropped a bit of bread
onto a pond below.

  The man was silent for a bit,
stunned of language,
then said to himself
It wasn't me! and then
It was an accident!
He put his tingling fingers to his face
and felt his head again—down
to the neck—before he made
his sobering descent.

(2)
It spun down
like a dragonfly
wing, pin-wheeling
in silence behind
its victim—he never
knew what hit him.
He was young,
an actor.
He was going to his
bank machine first,
then rehearsal for a play
he'd finally made it into.
Should this man
have known the final
fact about himself?
His head was severed
by a two-by-four
that fell from a
construction site.
He had read in high school

*

about the guillotine—
the Queen of France
flung in a pit
with her head face up
between her knees.

What would this boy
have thought, sitting
in the back of class,
laughing, passing notes,
if the words had flashed
out of his textbook:
This means you
or if the note he opened
had read: *It will sail*
in from behind, like
a pin-wheel, or a dragonfly
wing. Be comforted—
you won't feel a thing.

NIGHTMARE

I gave up tenure, transferred to my alma mater.
But they didn't like me there,
the students snarling, the Dean
appearing at my door as I was dressing.

He gave me a warning, listed all my short-
comings, raised the specter of old age
in the gutter. Then I was dragging
a rosary with beads the size of bowling
balls, was shedding clothes in the bed
of my old lover, trying to think of lessons
that would placate sneering freshmen.

Awake, the day seemed sinister, light
powerless to dissipate the fear of ragged old age:
me, a monument of miscalculations, bad
investments—and life too short now
for change. It looms, the smell and noise
of bad planning: watery potatoes, lumpy bed,
the bloom of plastic flowers.

OLD BOY

You had your way with budgets and with girls
in Alma Mater's gently flowing swirls;

the coeds you seduced with boasting tales
of drunken Irish poets, and the gales

of wit you matched with them in Dublin's pubs
(where, truth to tell, you swilled to quell their snubs).

And so you exercised reflected power
to find some likely coed to devour.

You and your fellow academic hounds
ran all the birds with broken wings to ground.

You built your little kingdoms in the tower
to hide your lack of intellectual power.

You hardly wrote a word, and when you did,
you never got a publisher to bid.

The canon's spared your imitating lore
of tragic, gifted geniuses ignored.

You bribed a friend to bring your book to light
but God is just—and so it died of fright.

And now you're gray, your chin is sagging low,
your jeans were handsome fifty years ago.

And now the boys are laughing at your shanks,
the coeds snigger at your classroom pranks:

you read the sexy scenes from Joyce aloud
as if to read were to be *so endowed*.

You haven't noticed that your time is o'er,
that Fortune's wheel has dumped you on the floor.

Too dense to know enough to be ashamed
your literary-lion-hood's disclaimed.

They're worthless now, your yellowed page and tooth.
Make way, old man, for talent, and for youth.

BEFORE THEY WERE MEN

The cleaning lady's little boy
has nothing to do
but to sit on the sofa
with a toy car and a *Coca,*
while Mami cleans
the *gringa*'s house. Weary
of sitting, he wanders
to the bathroom, the shower curtain
covered with drawings of dogs.
Mira, Mami! Perros!
His eyes—rising suns.
He runs to the kitchen
where she scrubs the sink,
pulls at her, pointing,
bounding like a pooch,
his day a sudden wonder,
so young, so willing
to be pleased.

STARLING ROAD

(1)

On Starling Road the families, intact
and kindly, gathered in the evenings on
their pillowed lawns. An old-gold evening sun
stroked cats who strolled from palm to palm, resting
in ligustrum hedges or stretching on
magnolia trunks in glossy arcs. The kids
seemed not to dash or run, but glide along
the asphalt softening in the heat, heads bent
and flashing in the sun. The youngest ones
pumped down the road on tricyles, with moms
in tow. We loved the shuffling fronds above
our heads, the pools behind our homes. Citrus
dropped off trees like ancient fantasies
of abundance: tangerines, Parson Browns, limes
and grapefruit fell uneaten in the grass.
No robbers came, no naughty kids grew up
there—not even traffic moved above a crawl.
The neighbors, in an evening ritual,
would greet each other on that cradle road,
the lush green, gold-flecked breast of Starling Road.

(2)

Across the street and up from us lived Phil
and Eleanor. They had a boy and girl
named Mark and Donna—fixtures in the yard—
who had a lonely air because there were
no peers precisely either age (eight or
nine, nine or ten) to play with. They followed
after teenagers, and babies in their
strollers, but mostly played alone or with
each other. They had a dog named Snowbell—

*

75

a poodle-ette with dirty paws and the foolish,
jolly face of growing puppies.
Donna in particular would dog our
steps and call to us to "come see this," or
"look what I can do," before the cartwheel
or the dog-entangled summersault. I
wished I could oblige those kids by being
twelve years younger—Mark and Donna had
a winning melancholy. Sometimes I'd give
in and chase them screaming, barking through
the yards, up one side of Starling Road and down
the other, until I saw myself: a
woman in a dress and high-heeled sandals
acting silly. I'd leave them suddenly,
leave them wondering what they did to make
me go away. I see their slight figures
in the yard, and hear their "please, please, please"
like distant chickadees at my back. "Please come back!"

(3)
Alternating with their rounds of school
and boredom and "Go play outside," was the
thrill of the unexpected: Eleanor
was a woman given to drama. She
had a gift for hauling in the doubters
and rounding up support for sudden schemes.
Phil, bemused, would go along, but the kids
would explode in their enthusiasm:
"Guess what we're going to do! We're going to be
colonials, and wear knickerbockers
and bonnets! My mom is making outfits
for us all!" And sure enough, in front of
their house appeared the Liberty Bell on
a trailer. Every weekend for a year we'd
see them troop out in their costumes to drive

the bell to local shopping malls, churches
and VFW halls. Even Snowbell
had a cunning tricorn cap with ear-hole.
I see Eleanor, her busy, frantic
face beneath a laced mobcap slapping at
the kids for screaming, jumping, walking on
her train, tense with significance and fear
her kids would misbehave, the car not start.
That Hallowe'en, when Mark and Donna came
to the door for chocolate kisses,
their costumes were out at the knee, hems down, frayed,
like tiny refugees from Valley Forge.

(4)
Even so, what could have prepared the souls
of Starling Road for this catastrophe?
One afternoon in spring the kids came home
from school, Killarney Elementary School,
to be killed by their waiting mother. She
killed herself as well, and Snowbell, too. We
never knew why; Eleanor shot them all.
Did she hide the gun, so not to
frighten them, and send them to their rooms to wait?
They might have thought they got in trouble
for neglecting chores or homework, pesky
tasks that hover over childhood—perhaps
they sulked. Or she might have done it better—
she might have made them snacks and had them play
quietly alone. At the worst, the one,
Mark, perhaps, may have heard the shot that killed
his sister, or the reverse. Donna may
have heard her brother's bullet, and held her
Snowbell to her heart, and wondered if the
thumping in her chest was what she heard,

*

77

before her mother came into the room
with tears and eyes that said *we can't go back
now, we're committed*.

 Phil found them in their
beds like pearls, each in a red shell. Snowbell
lay in Donna's arms like her own true child.

(5)
One might think the neighborhood that held us
all for decades in its yellow shawl of
light, its wax-white gardenia-verbena-
scented air, would not recover from a
traitor: no alarm exists to warn a
child from its mother. How could this be
home, that has a mark like Pilate's unwashed
hands? Or Cain, the bloody Cain? My parents
left the old homestead a few years later—
the pool, the trees—too much with kids grown up
and gone away. Their condo complex is
lovely in it way: the lakes, the lawns, the
same unsilted, winelike air and light that
falls on dogs and guns and kids alike. While
Starling Road remains, its pastel houses
still recline on beds of green Bermuda
grass beneath the torpid sky: empty, white.

HE SUMMONED THE TWELVE

and gave them the skill
to drive out demons by a word. He taught them
to cure every ill they came across:
palsy, dog bite, leprosy,
even horse fever and diseases of evil pleasure:
pox and the bloody rectum—
ills the rest of the rabbis claimed were
God's measure of wrath against Sodom
and Gomorrah.
Peter argued with the Rabbi:
Best and worst get equal cures?
Peter spit in the coals: *Not me.*
Perer peered at the brethren—
The cost of unnatural sin is death!
Peter planted his scaly hands on his thighs:
What kind of rabbi do you want me to be?
Peter's boast floated over the brethen. They nodded:
there's no cure for some things.

But the Rabbi took Peter in his arms,
the way a mother will take up her simple child,
or a man his lover: *I forgive you*
he murmured, as if Peter's mind was on
wielding his cock in the shadows, crowing
over boys and bad women.
The Rabbi kissed Peter's stricken, guilty face:
Make them all well, he said,
for your own sake.

PRECENTRIX

PRECENTRIX
(May be chanted to Gregorian tones 1.1 and 2.1)

1.1
Antiphon: No one should be so high and not be moving.
    There is no place to move.

When I was a young woman, I lived in New York City;
    I had a sugar daddy.
He was not a lecher—he was simply vain;
    He wanted to do the town with a charming girl on his arm.
He would take me anywhere; he would buy me anything.
    He bought me clothes at Bendel's and jewelry at Tiffany.
He had no taste, so I chose all the restaurants:
    Café des Artistes, Le Cirque, The Pierre, the Oak Room at the Plaza;

On my 28th birthday,
he took me to Windows on the World.
    Chic people found it slightly vulgar, overdone: a guilty pleasure.

He had gone to some trouble;
He had reserved a window table—the best seat in the house.
    the windows were low; the view of New York Harbor spectacular.

But I was frightened;
Fear was on the menu
    Great height is like a seasoning; one must decide how much one wants.

My taste for fear was bland; I never liked a thrill
    The Maître d' moved us to a banquette in the back.

The servers were all in white
with gold buttons and gold epaulettes
    They were like officers of a ship cruising in heaven.
*

They lavished us with attention;
the food was divine
    like ambrosia in nectar.

I felt contented as only the rich, the pampered, the loved can feel content;
    the atmosphere was hushed, as though the view itself was a
    manifestation of God.

But underneath—
106 stories underneath
was column of danger.

We knew—we all knew—it was dangerous.
That's why it was so expensive.

No one should be so high and not be moving;
There is no place to move.

Down was the flavor of the wine;
Down was the taste of the hors d'oeuvres
    Down was the savory lobster and the pheasant in truffle paste.

Down makes highness possible.
Down makes everything acute.

2.1
O Grief, you come unannounced
    not wih eyes cast down.

Not a shrouded goddess sad and final,
    But like a mountain lion.

Your red-ringed eyes are fixed on us.
    you never blink your eyes.

You know that we belong to you
       You know we cannot flee from you.

We go about our business;
the sky is blue; the day is beautiful,
       But Grief is stalking us.

Sudden One, you pounce on us
       Then we die, or we live in grief.

Thousands ate their breakfasts,
       thousands took the subway;

Thousands got to work on time,
       thousands organized their day.

Thousands did not see you, Grief
       Thousands did not hear your step,

Sudden One, you pounced on them;
       Millions heard you roar.

1.1
I saw a bumper sticker on a Subaru;
       it said: *If you want to work for peace, work for justice.*

I saw a film from Lebanon;
It was about the attacks on the Twin Towers;
       in it, an American and a Lebanese have a conversation.

The Lebanese is a man named Zabian.
He is gazing into the Mediterranean Sea;
       When the American emerges fron the water like Neptune.
                              *

He is a G.I. who has returned from the dead.
He was killed in nineteen eighty-three
When the Islamic Jihad blew up Marine barracks in Beirut.

He is not angry; He greets Zabian like a brother;
Neither is Zabian surprised to be greeted by the dead.

They talk of Nine-eleven;
they shake their heads and drop their eyes.
The sea washes their feet with its eternal tongue.

The G.I. says I know why they killed me.
I was a soldier. I fought like a soldier.
But why did they kill the people in the towers?

They were innocent;
they were working. They were not soldiers.
They were supporting their families like everyone else in the world.

Zabian looked at this boy in amazement;
As if to say, How could you be so ignorant?
Has your death taught you nothing?

He said: Young man, in this part of the world we cannot vote;
We cannot choose our leaders.

If they are cruel, if they are greedy, if they are murderous;
we are their first victims.

But you live in a democracy.
You choose your leaders.
The terrible power of the greatest nation lies in your people's hands.

If your leaders exploit us,
If they are greedy; if they mine the world for oil so that you can drive

your cars;
     your people are responsible.

If they empty the world of its riches;
so that you may be rich;
     your people are responsible.

If our children are like dwarves in the mud
so your children can be great
     your people are responsible.

You chose them. You loosed them on the world. You approved of their actions.
     You did not stop them. Your people are responsible.

The G.I. sat in silence, grieving in his fatigues;
     The sea was blue and passive.

We who live must think about the dead
     must read the glyphs of their falling bodies.

Gordy Aamoth the Alpha, Igor Zuckelman the Omega
     Hundreds and hundreds fell between them.

The air received them, the earth received them
     The fire received them.

These dead will not return from the dead
     they are bound to us and to each other in tragedy.

May the benevolent powers of the universe
     Grant us wisdom.

TWENTY YOUNG MEN

Ten men are dressed in orange prison suits,
their hands bound behind their backs,
ten more in black uniforms, faces
swathed in black scarves. Each man
is matched with another, orange, black
orange, black as they march
in sand along the shore or a silent sea.
The men in orange kneel, each black-
clad man standing behind with a knife.
We fear the worst and, in this universe
the worst happens.
          But in that other place, the place
of peace, the men in black drop their knives
and throw their masks into the sand.
They unbind their brothers
and help them step out of the prison
suits. They shed forever their black
uniforms. Now twenty young men
stand nude in the bright sun.
They turn to the sparkling sea
and run into the water, each man
diving and splashing until he is cool
and refreshed. They help each other
onto the shore and into the shade,
share tea and sugar dates, discuss
their future plans: a marriage, an import-
export business, a wing on the house
for an old parent, for children.
They say: I would like to know more
about you, who are so much like me.

FROM AN AIRPLANE WINDOW

So deep, deep down over Maryland.
Am I passing over the old green house
at Piney Point? Can our orange cat, Elmer,
or Grandma steaming crabs in the kitchen,
can my mom in the hammock under the mimosa tree
reading *The Saturday Evening Post*
or Gramp on the porch humphing over a hand of canasta,
and that gang of kids in the dinghy at the old dock
lolling into Chesapeake Bay—
can all that holds me close
be this far away?
I think I ought to know these things,
like the moment Andrew died,
my flesh and blood,
my own little future. Did I,
did I rub my eyes
or pick threads from my sleeve
when he died? And could I look down
on the earth, earth like the surface of skin,
and not know I hover over home?

ANOTHER STORY

A man is driving through the pine woods
that line a shimmering lake.
Docks and boats embroider the shore
like the fringe of a shawl, summer houses
tucked behind bending conifers. In the shallows
children with plastic buckets collect colored stones.
The sudden roar they hear—the man in the car,
the children on the shore—is like a locomotive
running amok through the woods.

I am the man's wife. I always fear
bad things will happen when he is out
of my sight. He calls it my tragic
imagination—but this time I'm right.
The entire side of a mountain loosens its grip,
collapses onto the road, the woods, the houses,
the boats, the children—fills the lake
with sludge. It happens so fast no one screams
or turns to point to the hills they have loved
so long. Mud embraces everyone.

This is where the story seems doubtful:
My husband's car has run out of gas,
sputtering to a stop two hundred yards
from where the mud will slide. He was cursing
his luck, getting out of the car and kicking it
when the ominous rumble came, as if
he had kicked the mountain itself and it fell.

Whin I listened to his story on the phone,
his voice pitched too high, his breath short,
I could feel his hand trembling in my own.

I'm making this up, because there must
always be two hundred yards between him
and disaster. He was never on that road,
not in recent years. But what are years
to mountains? What happens to others—
Powerball, the fallen rock—could happen to us all.

I'VE BEEN LISTED

in that heavenly book,
gold black heavy
shimmering under the hand
of the recording angel spirit
in paradise *cielo* across the water
on that grassy river bank
that waits for me with my mama
on the other side or my grandma
or disembodied spirits I will somehow
know are my mama, my grandma,
my favorite aunt with toll house
cookies or a beer.

Lord, I'm out here on your word—
in this weary world school of hard
knocks paying my dues taking
my hits giving as good as I get sinner
that I am goofing off loafing on my elbow
with the nonchalance of boys certain
of a good dinner girls birds
cats dogs squirrels I watch the other
side of the window the leaves fall
like red snow rain plankton floating
in the current of time like an ever-
flowing Jordan Lethe Mississippi.

Lord, I got my religion in time—
before Armageddon the second coming
all washed in the blood of the Lamb
Saint Sebastian punctuated with arrows
weeping Mary, Mary, and Mary
Santa Lucia with her plate of eyes
and me a day late, a dollar short but

Yes, Lord, I got my religion in time
before Gabriel blasts that golden horn
and the last train pulls out leaving
the despairing *sola*, *abandonata*,
weeping, crying, saying they're sorry
slumped on the sofa staring at *The Price*
Is Right, munching french fries,
until the end of time.

THE DAY NO ONE DIED

THE CRADLE

Where will you lay your baby down, young mother,
so tired, so worried?
Where will you lay your treasure down,
your fragile treasure?
This child, so tiny, so weak now, will burst into light.

Here is the haven we made for you, mother,
so quiet, so lovely.
In these arms lay your baby down,
this sacred treasure.
Our arms are the cradle to cradle our child of light.

TO THE SAUDI STUDENT WHO LEFT
HIS PRAYER SCHEDULE BEHIND

When he arrived in September he could say "hello"
and smile with eyes one might have seen
in a *caravanserai* a thousand years ago.
He would leave his shoes outside his bedroom
door, wear perfume in his hair, excuse himself
from the table to pray on a carpet on the floor,
guided by his compass and a yellow schedule.
I taught him how to grill a cheese sandwich,
boil pasta, fry an egg, so he could feed himself
when I was at work. His mothers and sisters
had fed him in Jiddah, and washed his clothes,
so I showed him how to do laundry, empty the trash,
sew on a button. His buddies came over
to practice English, smoke *sheeshas*—apple
tobacco flavoring the air. Their mothers
sent them spices and recipes for *kapsah*;
I showed them how to thaw the chicken,
steam the rice. He called me his American mother,
because there is no word in Arabic for a single woman
who owns a home, or drives a car to teach
at a university. His four mothers sent him sugar dates,
almonds and green coffee. They sent me a pound
of saffron. At Christmas I gave him a snow globe
of Santa Claus. He asked to come to church with me,
but lost his courage. He went home at Easter,
returned with a pink *hajalib* for me, his third mother
proud to have found a dress large enough
to fit such a big American woman.

INNAUGURATION DAY: 1/20/09

Children of a certain age remember
when White Only fountains stood
side by side at the Qwik Check
and Piggly Wiggly with Colored Only
fountains: machines equally chrome,
each with its wooden box
for short people to stand on.
All we kids supposed elixir
particular to those others
flowed inside. We sneaked away
from our mothers for a quick slurp,
only to dash back—astonished!
Hey, Mom! It's the same water as ours!

And what could Mother answer?

No matter her color, living down
in Colored Town or up
in Sigsbee Park, what should she say?
White folks are mean?
or should she say
Black folks are dirty?
They dammed the poison
best they could: *It's just the way
it's always been*, they told us.

Until today—this bright, cold day
we none of us thought to see
even in a new century. Today
we all drank (so thirsty!)
one water
from a single font.

CONSOLATION

Andrew had been dead three years when
a man from Accra, Ghana visited the convent.
His daughter was being clothed in the white habit
of the order. He wore a drape of kente cloth

across his chest like the sharp African sunset
or flaming dawn. He showed us how to pour libations.
One uses spirits, not beer or wine. One uses earth,
not sinks or paper cups. Each one in the circle

must drink. We sloshed vodka in the dahlia bed,
he prayed in Ashanti, then we each took a swig
to lead his tribal forebears to our convent.
I wore a habit I had sewn myself: a length

of wrinkle-free polyester from common stock,
the black cincture wrapped twice around my waist.
His daughter had crocheted it for me, her black
fingers so fast they could dye cloth, make beds,

pound cassava and bury the dead in a single
afternoon. Andrew gone three years now, I enclosed
in St. Helena's for two, a novice still. After
the service we sat on the verandah, this man from Ghana

and myself, quiet in the swirl of celebration, my sorrow
like a corpse between us. "How do your ancestors find you?"
I asked. "Do they fly behind the plane? Do they cross
the sea?" He was old, his skin like roasted eggplant.

They follow, he said. "But what if they're children,
what if they're only five?" I cried and poured
my story out. He listened with that kindly pity
they reserve for us—young, well-meaning, ignorant.

Andrew is in school, he told me. *Death does not dismiss
the truant from his lessons.* That little rascal, I thought.
*He must still grow to be a man, Sister Sharon. Learn
to trust your elders.* Then Grandma Helen was back

in the kitchen at Piney Point, in those happy summers,
making crab cakes, baking brownies. She sits Andrew down
at the table by the window sill. She scoots in his chair.
She opens his notebook to a fresh page. She sharpens his pencil.

GOSPEL COIN

It sparkles through green fingers of grass—
a silver dollar! But when I snatch it
from earth's hand, I am rebuked:
WHERE WILL YOU SPEND
ETERNITY? John 3:36.
Some punning evangelist tricked me
with aluminum lucre alongside the road—
a Johnny Apostle-seed luring sinners
with Caesar's dues.

I find a few more coins in the dirt
as I walk along, eyes cast down,
following where the missioner
must have driven in his white truck,
broadcasting coins out the window.
They jangle in my hand like the truth—
and I have to admit, I like something free.

But where can I spend the money?
Is there a Mercy Boutique,
a Forgiveness Five-and-Dime?
Show me the way to Salvation Mall.
Show me the Kingdom of Abundance!
My pocket is full of gospel coins
to spend in Eternity.

VISIT TO SUNSET HOME

Yes, that's me in the photo, sweetheart,
though it's hard to believe. My feet,
in patent leather pumps, once flashed
their grosgrain bows at Roseland,
my taffeta dress swirled to "Take the A Train."
It's a song by Benny Goodman, sweetie.
He played the clarinet. Now I wear
this workout suit your mother bought me
at the Bon Marché before my knees
gave out—two Gordian knots
a knife can't solve. Did you study
Alexander the Great? No, dear, he didn't play
at Roseland—that was a ragtime band.

> *My curls, long since cropped*
> *and gray; I sway on swollen ankles.*
> *My spine—the pylon, that wonder wand—*
> *collapsed upon itself, un-mortared bricks.*
> *I cannot take baths, the tub a lifetime*
> *away, in the land of glistening children,*
> *loose baby teeth. I have lost my teeth*
> *another way. Yet I do my workout every*
> *day: wake and thank the sun for rising, haul*
> *and shamble from my bed and down*
> *the hall. I pay my bills. I answer mail,*
> *my cursive waver echoes, like my face,*
> *what once it was.*

What's that, sweetie? Yes, that's Grandpa in uniform.
World War II was the one Grandpa fought in,
though he was in the Navy, thank God.
Did he tell you about the quartermaster's supply ship,
Old Stewpot? When the captain ran over a downed pilot
they meant to rescue? No? Well, now.

*

There's a tragedy. Hard to believe such things
could happen, but it was war. No, Hon, I don't recall
the details. They're like that photo
there. A song, a dress. The rest is gone.

TITIAN IN GLASGOW

You stroll the galleries of the Kelvingrove—
so many enticing sights, but one face arrests you.
In The Adulteress Brought Before Christ
there are Pharisees, crowd, a satin-clad Jesus,
the sinner shimmering in white scarlet gown.
We all know the text like a thought balloon
above Christ's head: *You—who are without sin—*
cast the first stone! But the bystander who eyes you
from the picture plane is the face you remember,
a handsome dandy turned from the debate
and the Savior in shadows. His sidelong gaze
accuses you. What of? Sniggering at codpieces?
Gawping at the naked gods? Moseying past the treasures
spread before you? You—who want nothing more
tha esprsso and scones in the museum café,
magnets and mummies in the gift shop.

The Museum of Transport is more your style.
Racers, ice cream trucks, gypsy vans,
motorcycles, rocking bikes, a street
with old-time shops, the flickers, the cop
cars, the popcorn stand. You wander upstairs
to the models of ships—the Queen Mary,
The Queen Elizabeth. There before you, in a mural
of the Clydeside shipyards, stands a painted welder
in his coveralls, hood pushed back—and there's that face
once more, that same Titian dandy, handsome,
gimlet-eyes. *You again*, he has crossed the centuries to say,
daydreaming while sins are judged and mighty ships are made.
Aye, you say. And when I've had enough of gods and monuments,
my handsome Titian friend, the coffee shop is that-a-way.

WOMAN AT THE WELL

You have to take one boyfriend after another
just to get along. Good women turn their noses up
at you so much you have to draw your water
in the heat of noon
instead of the cool morning
or the shady afternoon.

So there you are, walking a wide circle around judgment
when a Jew comes through the curtain
of heat, asks for a drink—so you think
Why is he talking to a Samaritan?
Let a Jewess haul his water,
since they think they're so smart.

But he argues, says if I knew who
he was I'd have all the water
I'd ever want for life. What a line!
But I like this guy—he's got one
of those good-natured smiles
in spite of the bushwah.
So I haul some up, gab a bit while
he drinks—it's been a while
since I've had a good chat.

OK, say I, *give me some magic water!*
and we laugh but he says, *Go get your husband*
—so he can have some, too, I suppose.
Don't got one, say I—and this guy laughs
right at me, says *You bet not—you've had five,*
not counting the one lying on your rugs right now.
Say! It's like he's spied on me
all my life—but likes me anyway.

So we back-and-forth about Jacob's well.
I say how nothing can be greater
than water in this weather; he tells me
I'm ignorant—I'd better wise up. Hey!
I don't take that guff from anyone!
But he looks me straight in the eye,
suddenly—like water himself, all wavery
in the heat and so bright. He's looking past
my past to a person complete.
I might have been a rabbi myself in another world or life.
This life. Did he say that? *This life.*
I know the Messiah's coming! I cry.

Did he nod? Did he say *It's me* straight out?
Ot did I see in his face that I'm right,
that the time is now,
that the water rising up through my bones
is the word?
I drop my jug, snatch up
my life, run to town
filled with the good news.

THE OUTHOUSE AT THE TOP OF THE WORLD

       is where all nature meets: the clean scent
of sage as you walk there, through wild flowers
(purple lupine, yellow gorse, white yarrow)
under the shadow of towering boulders, the small
rabbit dashing away as you unlatch the door,
prop it open to the massive Montana sky.
You sit there watching sculptured clouds
on their slow parade, listen to bawling
cattle as they wander over grass without
end—black dots scattered on gray-green
hills. You gaze at ranks of mountains marching
over the curve of the earth.

       Your reliable body, predictable as rain,
cycles through its daily seasons like the birds
that whistle around you, though they don't know
tonight the earth will turn, show you a black landscape
of stars and planets, that you will leave tomorrow,
that your days here are finished.

       You re-latch the door, praise the creator,
press the scented sage with your feet as you walk away.

THE DAY NO ONE DIED

There are seven billion people in the world.
Every second—every millisecond—thousands die
like drops of water rushing together
over a vast falls.
But on this particular day,
the old ladies gasping on mats in the corner of huts
or in hospices and hospitals, and the old men gazing at the ceiling
from their death beds, lived to see the sun rise once again.
Pedestrians walked safely down the sidewalks of the world,
and drunk drivers plowed into snow banks or hedges
instead of people or trees. Skiers also avoided trees,
and no boys hoping for paradise wrapped themselves in dynamite
to haunt the marketplaces of Afghanistan or Syria
or Iraq. Mothers all over the world selected apples and coconuts,
mangos and pomegranates to take home on what seemed like a normal day.
But on this particular day, the epidemiologists
had a few more hours to unravel the secrets of Ebola, HIV/AIDS,
malaria. The little boy, alone in a sterile room in Liberia
could look through the plastic window at his mother for one more day.
No one noticed this miracle—the ICU nurse simply noticed
that all of her patients seemed to rally a little, and the hospice
volunteer went from bed to bed smiling into the quiet faces
of those who waited, some with hope, others—on this particular day—
with less resentment than usual.
City morgues caught up on their backlogs
because, as sometimes happens, there were no
murders on this particular day, and no kids falling out of windows
or into ponds or out of cribs, no dads slipping on ice
or falling off ladders stringing lights or clearing gutters. Firemen
ate lasagna and were grateful for an uneventful day.
Far away, in those places we send soldiers
but never go ourselves, everyone seemed

*

to just sit down and smoke a cigarette, or a pipe,
or a hookah, and have a cup of coffee.
They all seemed to be waiting—waiting
for something all of them wanted.
On this particular day, everyone lived.

SHARON CUMBERLAND is Professor of English at Seattle University where she has taught since 1994. She directed its Creative Writing Program from 2007 to 2014. Raised in the Episcopal Church, she lived at the Catholic Worker in New York City for one year and was a member of the Episcopal Order of St. Helena for three years. After a career in New York City as an arts manager at the Lincoln Center Theater Company, The Phoenix Theater Company, and the Metropolitan Opera, she taught English at Brooklyn Technical High School while earning a Ph.D. in English from the City University of New York. Her poems have been widely published, and she has won many awards. She lives in Seattle, Washington with her husband, the letterpress printer James T. Jones.